GREENWICH AND DARTFORD TRAMWAYS

including Eltham and Bexley

Robert J Harley

MP Middleton Press

First published April 1993

ISBN 1 873793 14 6

© Middleton Press 1993

Design - Deborah Goodridge

Published by Middleton Press
        Easebourne Lane
        Midhurst
        West Sussex
        GU29 9AZ
        Tel: (0730) 813169

Printed & bound by Biddles Ltd,
        Guildford and Kings Lynn

CONTENTS

INDEX

INTRODUCTION AND ACKNOWLEDGEMENTS

London was once the centre of a large tramway system which included lines serving the neighbouring counties of Kent, Surrey, Middlesex, Essex and Hertfordshire. This book deals with the trams in Greenwich, Woolwich, Eltham, Bexley, Erith and Dartford; further volumes are in active preparation covering other areas of the capital. The research for this book was particularly interesting for me as I was able to renew contact with the area of London where I grew up. Early memories of my first tram ride with my Mother were evoked by the photos of Well Hall Road, Eltham with its seemingly endless procession of tramcars gleaming in their red and cream livery.

The trams played an important part in the development of South London and even today they are remembered with much affection for the frequent services, cheap fares and their eccentricities such as the conduit method of

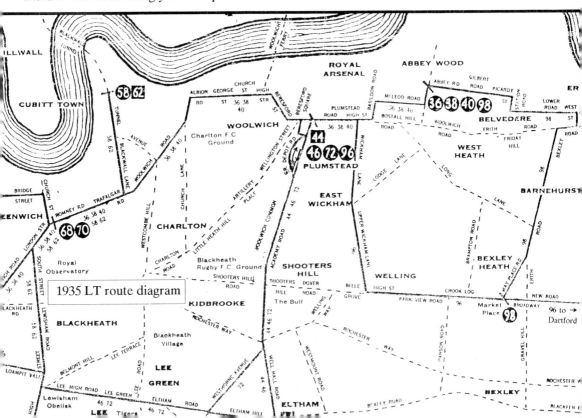

1935 LT route diagram

operation. In order to recreate this atmosphere of the past I am very indebted to those people who have contributed photos and information on the system.

Thanks are due especially to A.B.Cross, C.Carter, L.Dove, R.Elliott, J.C.Gillham, W.J.Haynes, J.H.Meredith, E.R.Oakley, The National Tramway Museum photographic collection (R.B.Parr, H.B.Priestley and R.J.S.Wiseman), A.D.Packer and K.H. Thorpe. Special thanks go to both Don Thompson and Alan Watkins for their help in preparing this book, also to John Wills for answering all my telephone enquiries so fully. Patricia Austin at the London Transport Museum gave me much assistance in locating post 1933 material.

GEOGRAPHICAL SETTING

Away from the banks of the River Thames the landscape of South East London and the adjoining area of North Kent is mostly hilly, due to the Thanet Beds. The land is fertile and before the spread of urbanisation was mostly devoted to farming and fruit growing. Quarrying has also been practised in the Dartford region and various local woodlands have supplied timber for the capital in the past.

HISTORICAL BACKGROUND

The ancient Roman road of Watling Street which ran from London to the Channel coast, forms the main axis of the area of this book. The River Thames was also a main artery of communication and ship-building thrived in Deptford and Woolwich. Greenwich Observatory stands on the Prime Meridian of the world; it is surrounded by a royal park and many fine buildings including the Naval College and the National Maritime Museum. The London and Greenwich Railway which was built on 878 arches, opened in 1836, thus providing London with its first commuter service. This became part of the South Eastern Railway which went on to establish the suburban railway network in the area which is still in operation today.

The Pimlico, Peckham and Greenwich Street Tramways Co. reached the area with a standard gauge horse line in 1871 and a narrow gauge (3ft. 6ins./1067mm.) horse tramway run by the Woolwich and South East London Tramways Co. was opened throughout from Plumstead to Greenwich in 1882. In 1888 the London County Council was formed and Woolwich and Greenwich were incorporated in the new county; Bexley, Erith and Dartford remained in the county of Kent. One of the many tasks confronting the new LCC was the acquisition of the old horse tramway companies and the substitution of a more up-to-date form of traction. In January 1904 a brand new electric tramway was opened from the "King William the Fourth" public house in

Trafalgar Road to the Thames bridges in central London. This line was constructed using the conduit method of current collection which was about twice as expensive to build as a conventional overhead wire tramway. The narrow gauge section through to Plumstead and eventually Abbey Wood took much longer to reconstruct mainly because of the problem of installing standard gauge tracks in very narrow streets.

Bexley Council Tramways were opened in October 1903 by the newly elected MP for Woolwich, Will Crooks. The Bexley lines extended from the Erith boundary at Northumberland Heath to a terminus adjoining the Woolwich horse tramway in Plumstead High Street; they were constructed to standard gauge and drew power from the usual overhead wire system.

In August 1905 the Erith Council Tramways commenced operations from Abbey Wood to Northumberland Heath and along a short branch line to Northend. The enthusiasm for electric traction was now unstoppable and Dartford Council joined the ranks of operators with lines from Bexleyheath to Horns Cross and Dartford Station to Wilmington. Shortly after the Dartford system opened in February 1906, plans were laid for a link up further east to the Gravesend Tramways at Swanscombe. However, the extension was never constructed and Horns Cross remained the eastern outpost of the London network.

In the county of London, even the wealthy LCC was getting concerned about the high costs of new conduit tramways, therefore, since Bexley Council had already brought overhead wires into the Borough of Woolwich, it was decided that the reconstructed horse tramway from Beresford Square to Abbey Wood should be similarly equipped. This section was opened in 1908 and a further new route was constructed southwards from Woolwich to terminate at Eltham High Street; this line opened in 1910. The LCC had to suffer yet another current collection problem with the Eltham route as the Astronomer Royal, based at Greenwich Observatory, objected to the use of a single wire overhead system which he claimed would affect the sensitive scientific instruments; he further stipulated that this method could not be used within a three mile radius of the Observatory. The LCC gave way graciously and constructed a fully insulated double trolley system similar to modern trolleybuses. Thus the citizens of Eltham were treated to a set up which was also employed at such exotic locations as Cincinnati, Ohio and Havana, Cuba! Slow progress was being made with the link from Woolwich to Greenwich and the through connection to central London was finally established in April 1914. After World War I the progressive LCC were still thinking in terms of expanding the system and to this end Eltham was linked with Lee Green in 1921. This was the final use of the double trolley, as the Royal Observatory moved from Greenwich in 1926 and the Eltham lines were converted to the normal single wire.

Much house building took place in the Eltham area and the estate bordering Westhorne Avenue was served by a new tramway running through from Well Hall Circus to the "Yorkshire Grey" public house. Operation commenced in June 1932. This proved to be London's last new tramway route and exactly one year later all public transport operations in the capital were transferred to the London Passenger Transport Board. The new owners of London's tramways set about the replacement of the system. The Wilmington route in Dartford was given over to buses in 1934 and most of the erstwhile Bexley, Erith and Dartford tramways were replaced by trolleybuses in 1935. World War II delayed further conversions and the trams finally disappeared in July 1952. The local trolleybuses did not last much longer and diesel buses replaced them in March 1959.

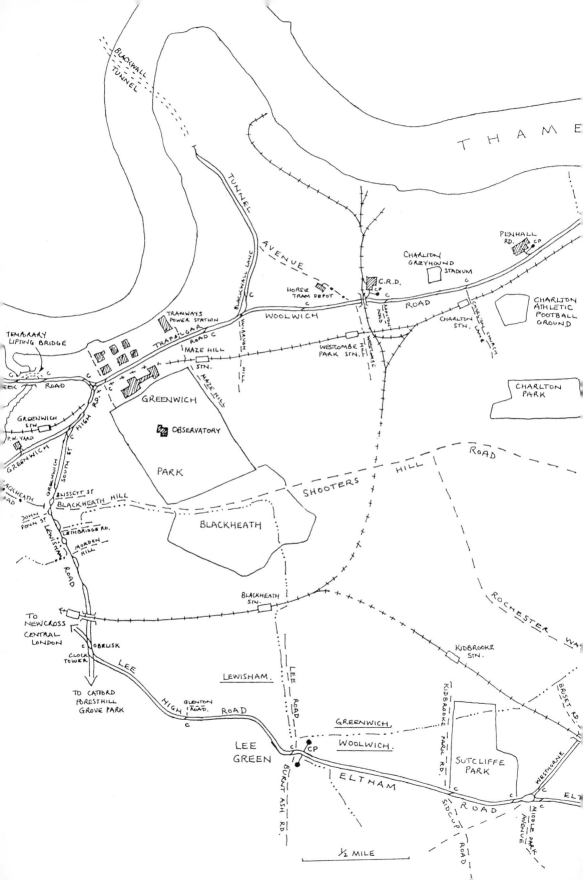

FREE FERRY

CP

ROYAL ARSENAL

LWICH CKYARD

WICH

CHURCH ST

HIGH ST

BERESFORD SQ.

OLWICH

CHAPEL ST

WOOLWICH DOCKYARD STN.

POWIS ST

C BERESFORD ST

C PLUMSTEAD

ROAD

PLUMSTEAD STN.

C

PARSONS HILL
T'BUS TURNING LOOP.

THOMAS ST

ANGLESEA ROAD

T'BUS REVERSING TRIANGLE

GRIFFIN RD.

GALLOSSON RD.

BARTH RD.

KASHGAR RD.

WOODHURST RD.

BASILDON RD.

MCL

WICH.

WOOLWICH.

ROYAL ARTILLERY BARRACKS

GRAND DEPOT RD.

WOOLWICH NEW RD.

WOOLWICH ARSENAL STN

LAKEDALE RD.

RIVERDALE RD

C

WICKHAM

WILTON EAST WILKINSON ROAD

BOSTALL HILL

BOSTA W

NIGHTINGALE PL.

PLUMSTEAD COMMON

R.M. ACADEMY

WOOLWICH COMMON

LANE

KING'S HIGHWAY

VILLACOURT RD.
T'BUS TURNING LOOP

WOOLWICH COMMON

ACADEMY ROAD

C

D WALK

ELTHAM COMMON

LONDON.
WOOLWICH.

KENT.
BEXLEY.

WELL HALL

WESTMOUNT

CASTLE WOOD

JACK WOOD

OXLEAS WOOD

DOVER RD.

WELLING STN.

UPPER WICKHAM LANE

BELLE

SANING RD.

GROVE ROAD

HIGH

C

WELL HALL ROAD

WELLING WAY

FALCONWOOD STN.

HAM HALL STN.

ELTHAM PARK STN.

ELTHAM PARK

ROCHESTER WAY

SHERARD RD.

HIGH ST

ROAD

OCP RD.

CE

LONDON.
WOOLWICH.

KENT.
CHISLEHURST AND SIDCUP

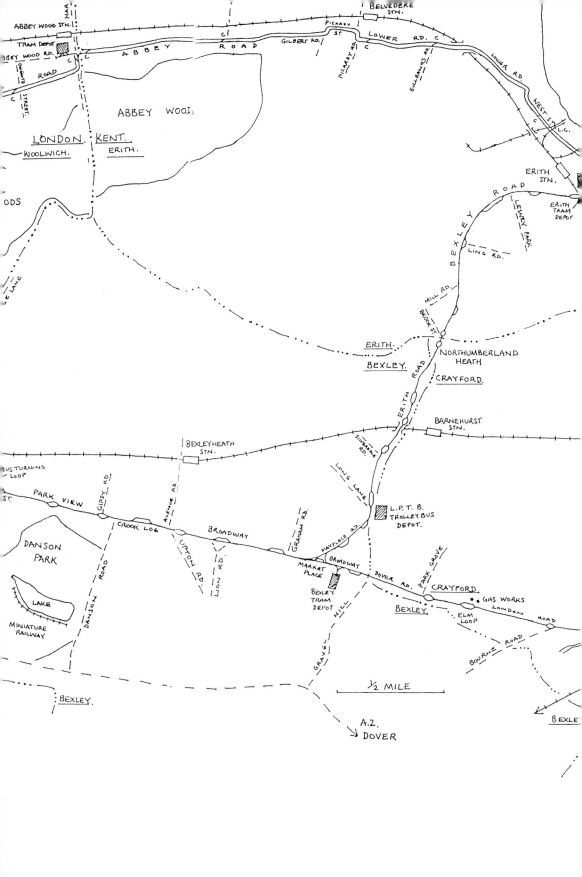

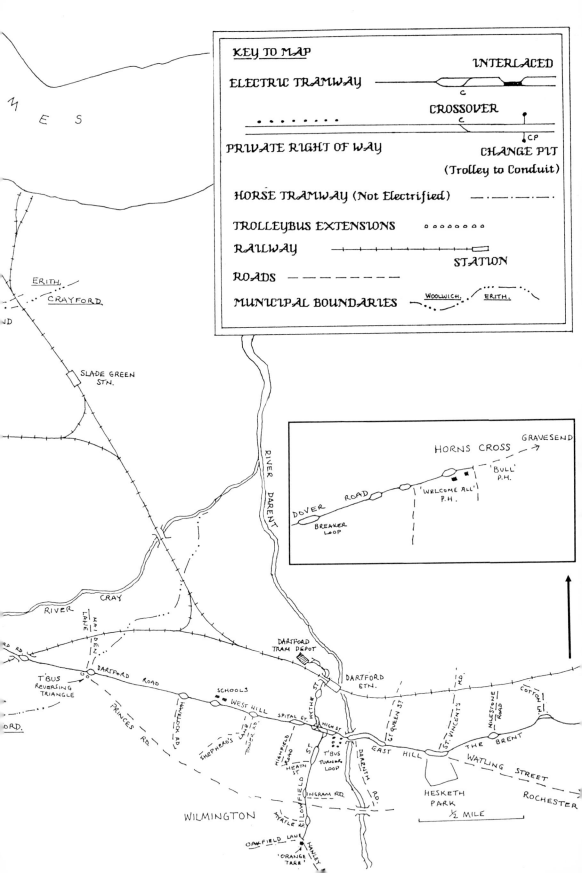

1. Blackheath Hill to Greenwich
BLACKHEATH HILL

1. Car 2 stands close to the borough boundary between Greenwich and Lewisham. It is on a workman special from Woolwich to Catford and is pictured here on Lewisham Road. The motorman peers from the front of the tram whilst the conductor is no doubt frantically trying to cram in everyone with exhortations of "Move down the car, please!" He will then press the bell twice and we're off! (D.A.Thompson)

2. Unusually for the post-war system, much of the route between Lewisham and Greenwich remained single track and loops. Here we see car 147, a trolleyless HR2 class car, on Orchard Hill loop. Note the number 776 painted on the section box which stands in front of the old style pedestrian crossing..no zebra stripes in those days! Note also the separate bus and tram stop signs and the silver and black Greenwich Borough Council sand and grit bin by the roadside. (R.J.Harley Coll.)

3. A tram waits patiently at the John Penn Street loop for an as yet unseen southbound car. Above the tram is suspended one of Greenwich's famous hanging street lamps. They could be lowered by a winch device on the lamp standard so that the globes could be cleaned. (D.A.Thompson)

4. Two cars on service 58 pass at the crossroads with the A2, Blackheath Hill. The driver of car 1891 seems to be unaware that the indicator box glass has fallen down, perhaps he thought it didn't matter on this fine, sunny day in May 1950. (John H. Meredith)

5. Service 58 was replaced by bus route 185 on Sunday 7th. October 1951. Not long before the end car 101 is seen on Greenwich South Steet with the clock tower of the town hall in the background. (R.J.Harley Coll.)

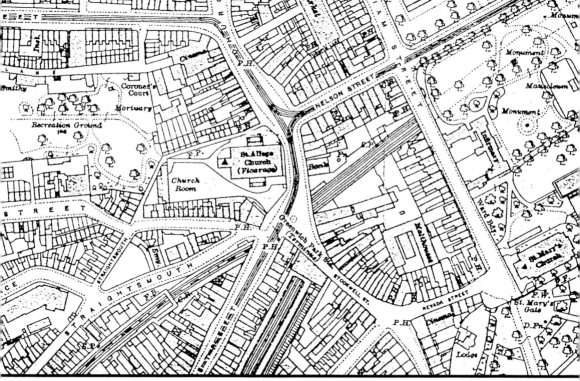

The 1916 map shows the tramway in London Street (lower centre) sandwiched between the ex-LCDR terminus (closed 1917) and the ex-SER North Kent line.

(lower left)

6. At the junction of South Street and Greenwich High Road, car 91, formerly owned by East Ham Corporation, pauses on a service 36 short working. Car 1874 picks up passengers as it prepares to join the "main line" London bound tracks. The sign marked "Architecture" refers to the Festival of Britain, Lansbury Development across the water in Poplar. This festival site was open from 3rd. May to 30th. September 1951. (R.J.Harley Coll.)

7. The sun is out and a young lady pushing a baby carriage turns round to look at the photographer in this early view of London Street, Greenwich. Car 139 still in near original condition with open top and reversed stairs, passes the Carlton Theatre en route for the metropolis. (R.J.Harley Coll.)

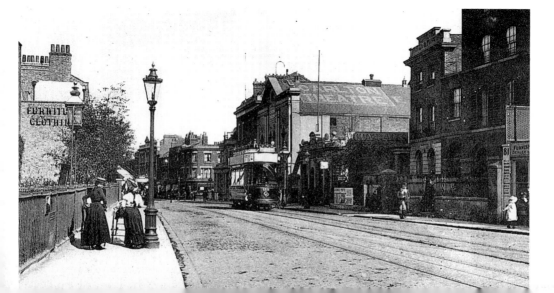

8. Towards the end of the tram era car 84 negotiates the single track with double conduit slots in Greenwich High Road formerly London Street. There is plenty of evidence of bomb damage and some former shops like the one housing the Midland Bank have been temporarily converted until building materials are available for new premises. (R.J.Harley Coll.)

9. The Parish Church of St.Alphege built by Nicholas Hawksmoor in the eighteenth century reputedly stands on the spot where Archbishop Alphege was murdered by the Danes in 1012. A contrast to the ordered Edwardian scene as LCC car 314, splendid in its maroon lake and cream livery, prepares to turn into Nelson Road. (R.J.Harley Coll.)

10. At the three way tramway junction of Greenwich High Road, Church Street and Nelson Road a tram carefully negotiates the crossings as it heads towards Blackwall Tunnel terminus. A father and his son who is attired in the traditional 1950s school cap, look up at the church which was gutted during the war and was awaiting restoration. (D.A.Thompson)

11. Greenwich Church Street was the terminus for routes 70 and 68 which then turned westward along Creek Road. Here car 589 is ready for departure; note the workmen's canvas hut and brazier in the background. (C.Carter)

12. The lifting bridge over Deptford Creek was rebuilt in 1949 and a temporary structure, seen here, was erected complete with double tram tracks equipped with conduit. It had a short life as part of a tram route because services 70 and 68 were replaced by buses in July 1951. The two dockland services will be described more fully in a future album. (C.Carter)

13. A handcart rests by the kerb as car 1879 approaches along Nelson Road. Appropriately for an area so steeped in naval tradition, the trams in the distance are in Romney Road which leads to Trafalgar Road. In 1992, aside from a vaste increase in modern traffic this scene has hardly changed in the intervening decades. (National Tramway Museum. H.B.Priestley)

14. There is plenty of activity in Trafalgar Road as a tram slows for the trailing crossover outside the "King William the Fourth" pub. In horse car days it was here that the grumbling passengers had to detram from a standard gauge London car to a narrow gauge Woolwich one. (D.A.Thompson)

2. Blackwall Tunnel Branch

15. Car 1892 turns out of Blackwall Lane on its journey to Victoria. This section of track to the Tunnel opened in May 1906; note the splayed arrangement of the tracks as they pass either side of a public convenience. (D.A.Thompson)

16. The trees, the pre-fabs and the gasometer in the distance somehow conjure up the atmosphere of post war South London. Car 1897 having discharged most of its passengers, rolls along Tunnel Avenue towards the end of the line. (National Tramway Museum. R.B.Parr)

17. The imposing entrance to Blackwall Tunnel dominates this view of the tram terminus where car 103 waits on the single track stub. The cafe on the right was sometimes used by crews to replenish the famous tram-drivers' tea-cans. Unfortunately the cafe and the tropical fish shop nextdoor disappeared in major highway developments in the 1960s and 1970s after the construction of a second tunnel and its associated approach roads. (C.Carter)

18. Looking south towards Greenwich from the terminus a Metropolitan Police phone box can be glimpsed behind car 149. The BBC TV series "Dr. Who" featured such a box transformed into a time and space vehicle. Whether the good Doctor had just materialised when this photo was taken is unlikely, however, there must be many who would like to turn back the clock and experience a ride on a 58 again! (L.Dove)

CHARLTON

19. During trailer experiments just before WWI, a standard LCC M class car poses with an ex-horse tram in tow at the entrance to Charlton Works. These experiments led to the use of trailers on certain lines including those to Eltham and Abbey Wood, however, in the long run the solution to improving the service lay in faster, more comfortable bogie cars and the trailer experiment fizzled out in the 1920s. (LCC official photograph)

20. Along Woolwich Road, Charlton, car 1953 has just passed under the railway bridge carrying the Angerstein Wharf goods only branch. On the right of the tram is the single track spur leading to the Central Repair Depot. (D.A.Thompson)

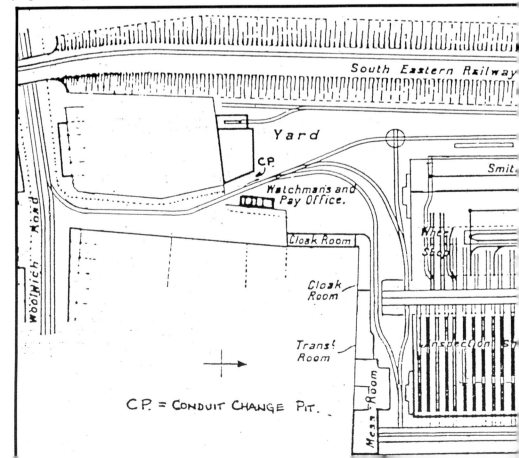

South Eastern Railway

Yard

C.P.

Watchman's and Pay Office.

Cloak Room

Cloak Room

Trans? Room

Woolwich Road

Smit.

Inspection Sh

Mess Room

C.P. = CONDUIT CHANGE PIT.

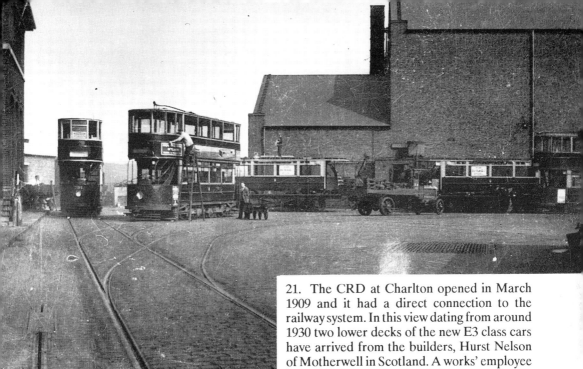

21. The CRD at Charlton opened in March 1909 and it had a direct connection to the railway system. In this view dating from around 1930 two lower decks of the new E3 class cars have arrived from the builders, Hurst Nelson of Motherwell in Scotland. A works' employee is perched on a cleaning ladder attending to the advert panel of an E1 class car. (R.J.Harley Coll.)

Central repair depot (L.C.C. Tramways) at Charlton - Original layout.

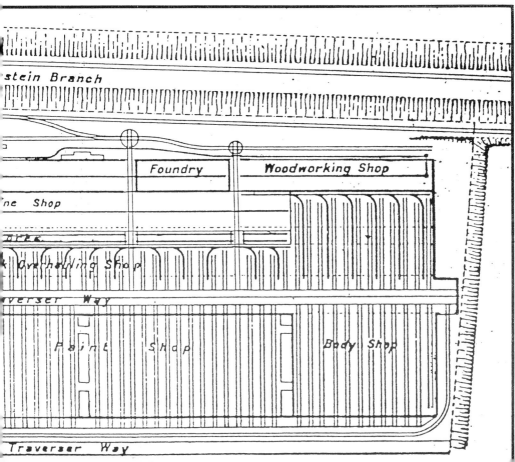

...stein Branch

Foundry   Woodworking Shop

...ne Shop

...rk.

...Overhauling Shop

...verser Way

Paint Shop   Body Shop

Traverser Way

22. Inside the repair shops everything was organised on a production line principle, ironically pre-dating the famous Henry Ford set up. The CRD was brought further up to date in 1929 and the whole lot passed to London Transport in 1933. Tramway repairs ceased on the closure of the system in 1952 and LT finally pulled out in 1959. The site was levelled for urban redevelopment in 1991. (LCC official photograph)

23. Car 91 leads a parade of electric traction through Charlton. This vista of solidly built terrace houses must have witnessed many lines of trams especially on match days when Charlton Athletic were playing at home. Crowds of over 50,000 were regularly transported to and from the Valley and the red and cream trams matched the favours of the supporters. (D.A.Thompson)

WOOLWICH

24. The Royal Dockyard at Woolwich was established by King Henry VIII in 1512. The tramtracks make an elegant curve beside its boundary walls. According to the clock on the Road Haulage Executive building it is just after 3 o'clock on a sunny afternoon. (D.A.Thompson)

ROUTE 36/38 | **Abbey Wood-Woolwich-New Cross-Elephant & Castle-Embankment** | P.M. times are in heavy figures

Via McLeod Rd., Basildon Rd., Plumstead High St., Plumstead Rd., Beresford St., Woolwich High St., Woolwich Church St., Woolwich Rd., Trafalgar Rd., Romney Rd., Nelson St., London St., Greenwich Rd., Deptford Broadway, New Cross Rd., Old Kent Rd., New Kent Rd., London Rd. Route 36 via Blackfriars Rd., Blackfriars Bridge, Victoria Embankment (return via Westminster Bridge, Westminster Bridge Rd.) Route 38 via Westminster Bridge Rd., Westminster Bridge, Victoria Embankment, Blackfriars Bridge., Blackfriars Rd.

RAILWAY STATIONS SERVED : Abbey Wood, Plumstead, near Woolwich Arsenal, Charlton, Greenwich, New Cross, New Cross Gate, Elephant & Castle, Blackfriars, Temple, Charing Cross, Westminster, near Waterloo, Lambeth North.

Service interval : EACH ROUTE. WEEKDAYS 6 mins. (Mon. to Fri. eve. 12 mins., Sat. eve. and morn. peak hours 8 mins.), SUNDAY 10 mins. (Additional peak hour service on Weekdays between Abbey Wood and New Cross every 8 mins.)

	WEEKDAYS	First			MON. FRI. Last		SAT. Last		SUNDAY	First	
	†	*	†	*	MF† S0†				*		† *	* †
ABBEY WOOD	...	...	..	..	4 35 5 29 5 41	10 10 10 16 11 30	10 11 10 16 11 30		.. 5 24		A6 2 5 58 7 13 7 28
Woolwich *Perrott Street*	...	...	..	4 48 5 42 5 54	10 23 10 29 11 43	10 23 10 29 11 43		5 37 5 49		6 8 6 11 7 26 7 41
Woolwich *Beresford Square*	...	...	..	4 50 5 44 5 56	10 25 10 31 11 45	10 26 10 31 11 45		5 39 5 51		6 10 6 13 7 28 7 43
Woolwich Road *Blackwall Lane*	4 17	...	..	5 5 5 59 6 11	10 40 10 46 12 0	10 42 10 47 12 0		‡5 50 5 55 6 6		6 25 6 28 7 43 7 58
New Cross Gate	4 32	4 42	5 4	5 16 5 20 6 14 6 26	10 55 11 1 12 15	10 57 11 2 12 15	4 12 6 1	.. 6 20 6 27		6 39 6 42 7 57 8 12
Elephant & Castle	4 48	4 58	5 20	5 32 5 36 6 30 6 42	11 11 11 17	11 12 11 17	4 27 6 16	.. 6 42		6 54 6 57 8 12 8 27
Blackfriars *John Carpenter Street*	..	5 7	..	5 41 5 45	11 20	11 20	4 35 6 24	...		7 5 8 19
EMBANKMENT *Savoy Street*	5 0	¶5 12	5 32	5 44 5 48 6 42 6 54	11 23 11 30	11 23 11 30	4 37	... 6 52		7 4 8 21 8 37

					†		†		†	†	† †
EMBANKMENT *Savoy Street*	...	5 0	¶5 14	5 44	...	10 35 10 42 11 23 11 30	10 35 10 42 11 23 11 30	4 38	.. 4 47 6 36 8 21		...
Blackfriars *John Carpenter Street*	..	5 3	5 20	...	10 45	11 33	10 45	11 33	4 40 4 43 4 49 6 38		...
Elephant & Castle	...	5 12	5 29	5 56	...	10 48 10 54 11 36 11 42	10 48 10 53 11 36 11 41	4 47 4 51 4 57 6 46 8 31		...
New Cross Gate	3 55	5 28	5 45	6 12	...	11 4 11 10 11 52 11 58	11 3 11 8 11 51 11 56	§5 7 5 6 5 12 7 1 8 46		...
Woolwich Road *Blackwall Lane*	4 10	5 43	6 0	6 27	...	11 19 11 25	11 18 11 23	... 5 20 5 26 7 15 9 0		...
Woolwich *Beresford Square*	4 25	5 58	6 15	6 42	...	11 34 11 40	11 34 11 39	... 5 35 5 41 7 30 9 15		...
Woolwich *Perrott Street*	4 27	6 0	6 17	6 44	...	11 36 11 42	11 36 11 41	... 5 37 5 43 7 32 9 17		...
ABBEY WOOD	4 40	6 13	6 30	6 57	...	11 49 11 55	11 49 11 54	... 5 50 7 45 9 30		...

SUNDAY—Last				SUNDAY—Last			
	*	†			*	†	
ABBEY WOOD	10 16 10 21 11 56	EMBANKMENT *Savoy Street*	10 44 11 0 11 24 11 30	A–Time at Wickham Lane.
Woolwich *Beresford Square*	10 31 10 36 12 11	Blackfriars *John Carpenter St.*	.. 11 2 .. 11 32	MF–Monday to Friday only.
Woolwich Road *Blackwall Lane*	10 46 10 51 12 26	Elephant & Castle	10 54 11 9 11 34 11 39	S0–Saturday only.
New Cross Gate	11 0 11 5 12 40	New Cross Gate	11 9 11 24 11 49 11 54	¶–Time at Charing Cross.
Elephant & Castle	11 15 11 20	Woolwich Road *Blackwall Lane*	11 23 11 38	‡–Time at Greenwich *Church.*
Blackfriars *John Carpenter St.*	11 22	Woolwich *Beresford Square*	11 38 11 53	§–Via Walworth Road.
EMBANKMENT *Savoy Street*	11 24 11 30	ABBEY WOOD	11 53 12 8	*–Via Blackfriars. †–Via Westminster

EARLY JOURNEYS : New Cross Gate to Blackwall Tunnel, WEEKDAYS at 4 41, 5 14, 5 21, MF5 29, S05 31, MF5 46, MF5 51 a.m.
Blackwall Tunnel to Waterloo Bridge, WEEKDAYS at 5 15*, MF5 40*, S05 37*, 5 49†, S05 57†, MF6 10* a.m.
Blackwall Tunnel to New Cross Gate at MF5 56, MF6 14 a.m.

25. On Woolwich High Street by Ferry Approach, car 2 has halted for the conductor to raise the trolley pole. The tram will then proceed up to the change pit. The triple overhead wires were erected for a wartime trolleybus extension in July 1943 to a new terminus at Parsons Hill. (C.Carter)

26. The motorman of car 1005 glances in the mirror to check that the conductor is back on board after stowing the trolley pole. The tram will then leave Woolwich change pit drawing power from the conduit. The driver could also have noticed the poster in the restaurant window advertising a three course lunch for two shillings, which is ten pence in modern currency! (C.Carter)

←

27. The conduit slot crosses to the centre of the London bound track and the plough is ready to be lifted and slid under the next tram. The conduit adjacent to the change pit was not "live" to protect the attendants; trams approached in both directions using the overhead. (John C. Gillham)

28. Not much traffic about as we look down Beresford Street towards the Square with the tram rails taking up most of the carriageway. Note the facing crossover which was used so that trams could go round vehicles or delivery vans parked by the left hand kerb. (John C. Gillham)

LINES AROUND
BERESFORD SQUARE

29. Holy Trinity Church at the corner of Beresford Street and the Square was demolished in 1962. A rather misty day just before the turn of the century sees a Woolwich and South East London Co. horse car unloading outside the church; the tram will then resume its leisurely trot on to Greenwich. The top deck passengers sit back to back on knifeboard seating. (R.J.Harley Coll.)

30. The Royal Arsenal Gates form the backdrop to this lunchtime scene of Arsenal workers crowding onto cars to get home for their midday meal. The Royal Arsenal was a hugh ordnance factory spread over many acres and employing over 80,000 people in wartime. No wonder that the LCC saw the provision of electric transport a priority for the Woolwich area. (R.J.Harley Coll.)

31. Some four years on from the previous photo and the electric cars have arrived. In this view dating from about 1909 a large crowd has assembled at 1:50 pm. Amongst the speakers is Will Crooks MP who was only the fourth Labour Member of Parliament to be elected. He served the Woolwich constituency from 1903 to 1921; he was a champion of the tramways and always used them to travel to political meetings. (R.J.Harley Coll.)

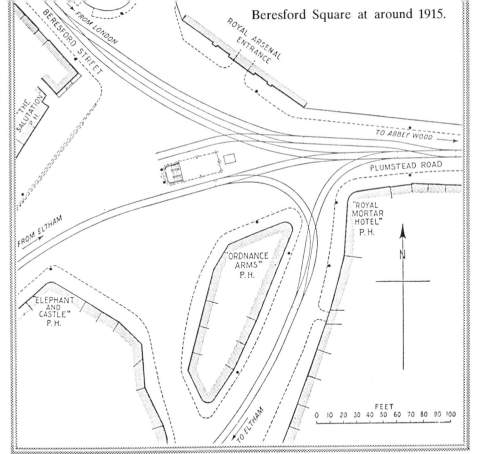

Beresford Square at around 1915.

FROM LONDON

BERESFORD STREET

THE SALUTATION P.H.

ROYAL ARSENAL ENTRANCE

TO ABBEY WOOD

PLUMSTEAD ROAD

FROM ELTHAM

"ROYAL MORTAR HOTEL" P.H.

"ORDNANCE ARMS" P.H.

N

"ELEPHANT AND CASTLE" P.H.

TO ELTHAM

FEET
0 10 20 30 40 50 60 70 80 90 100

32. Beresford Square was a destination well known to several generations of Londoners. The trams and the street market seemed to belong together and much of the life went out of the place when the tracks fell silent in July 1952. Here a car on service 40 approaches the policeman on point duty. It is to be hoped that the man in blue is not PC 288 Sidney Brandon who almost caused a strike amongst LT drivers in the early post war period. The constable seems to have had an aversion to trams and he would issue a summons for the most trivial traffic offence; honour was satisfied when he was transferred by his inspector to more "suitable duties!" (John C. Gillham)

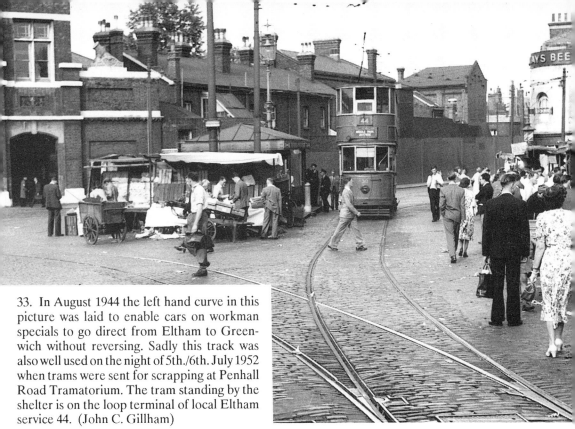

33. In August 1944 the left hand curve in this picture was laid to enable cars on workman specials to go direct from Eltham to Greenwich without reversing. Sadly this track was also well used on the night of 5th./6th. July 1952 when trams were sent for scrapping at Penhall Road Tramatorium. The tram standing by the shelter is on the loop terminal of local Eltham service 44. (John C. Gillham)

34. A westbound 38 swings across an unusually deserted Square. Note that the tram is taking power from the positive trolleybus wire; on the section between the Woolwich change pit and Plumstead the overhead was shared with the 696 and 698 trolleybus services. (D.A.Thompson)

35. Looking east this time, a tram proceeds into Plumstead Road whilst an inspector checks his timecard at the shelter where services 44, 46 and 72 terminated. (John C. Gillham)

36. A final view of the Arsenal Gate seen through the lens of Don Thompson who has stationed himself in Green's End and has captured car 169 passing an original LCC clover leaf tram stop. This tram was one of a batch built for Leyton Corporation which served with London Transport from 1933 to July 1952. It was burnt for scrap at Penhall Road late in 1952. (D.A.Thompson)

37. The clock on Manze's Eel and Pie Shop shows 5·45 pm on a summer's evening. In front of car 1275 is the interlaced point necessary for the sharp bend out of the Square and into Woolwich New Road. The tram pictured here was rehabilitated by LT in the 1930s as part of a restricted modernisation programme to keep the fleet going until trolleybus conversion. The LCC Tramways Trust are currently restoring a similar car for eventual operation at the National Tramway Museum. (C.Carter)

38. The last tram week and car 1861 accelerates out of the one way section of Woolwich New Road. Concealed behind the tram is the original 1910 substation built to supply current for the Eltham section. The building has survived, converted into a theatre and renamed the "Tramshed." (C.Carter)

39. Car 593 suitably daubed with last day epitaphs is captured on film at the bottom of Grand Depot Road where it rejoins the London bound tramtracks in Woolwich New Road. (National Tramway Museum. R.B.Parr)

40. At the end of December 1948 a former   the one way single track out of Woolwich.
West Ham Corporation car doggedly ascends   (National Tramway Museum. H.B.Priestley)

WOOLWICH COMMON

41. The part of Woolwich situated on the heights above the Thames belongs very much to the military tradition. St. George's Garrison Church and a line of horse chestnut trees act as a background to double trolley equipped car 1432 as it makes its way to Eltham shortly after the route was opened. (R.J.Harley Coll.)

42. This is the same corner as the previous picture, but seen in 1949. The inbound and outbound tracks separate here as is demonstrated by cars 1145 and 1092. The Royal Artillery Barracks behind the service 46 tram, were built in stages from 1775 to 1802 in a straight line of exactly a quarter of a mile in length. (D.A.Thompson)

43.   The double trolley arrangement can clearly be seen on car 1429 as it passes the Garrison Church. This place of worship was severly damaged in World War II and the shell of the building is now preserved. (R.J.Harley Coll.)

44. 29, The Common, Woolwich was the birthplace in 1833 of General Gordon of Khartoum. Car 302 passes this graceful row of houses where for many years a blue plaque marked General Gordon's home. Unfortunately in the 1970s in a piece of crass civic vandalism the whole row was pulled down and replaced by a hideous featureless development. (R.J.Harley Coll.)

45. Spring comes to Woolwich Common and the red and white warning flag of "Track Up" indicates that the permanent way department are doing some spring cleaning repairs of their own on Academy Road. Note the bent pole structure for taking current to power the road mending equipment. (C.Carter)

46. Woolwich Common remains to this day semi-rural in appearance. In 1910 the gates of the Royal Military Academy are about to be passed by LCC car 1436 as it toils up the hill. The Academy itself was founded in 1741 and rebuilt in 1806. Most of the splendid elm trees hereabouts survived until stricked by disease in the late 1960s; on this fine summer's day so many years ago, a line of baby carriages are positioned in the shade to the left of the tramcar. (R.J.Harley Coll.)

47. Just up the hill from the previous photograph no. 45, car 166 prepares to cross Shooters Hill Road. (C.Carter)

4. To Eltham and Lee Green
ELTHAM

DV 1756

L London Transport Trams
Return Journey only
Change at Elephant
St. George's Church and
Denmark Hill Station
Change at Greenwich Church

Marquis of Granby and Blackwall Tunl	Deptford Park Gate and Blackwall Tun
1	21
2	20
3	19
4	18
5	17
6	16
7	15
8	14a
	14
	13
	12

2½d Wk Ret

56 58
60 62
84

For conditions see back

48. The trams acquired by LT from Walthamstow Corporation were regarded as the fastest in the fleet. Here we see one member of the class, car 2046, showing its paces at the top end of Well Hall Road just past the "Welcome Inn." Shooters Hill police station is in the distance with a huddle of pre- fabs at its feet. (John H. Meredith)

49. A lady waits hopefully at the stop opposite Broad Walk as on the London bound track a tram convention assembles with coincidently car 2046 bringing up the rear. At all events there seems to be plenty of time for the crews to have a chat whilst the cause of the delay is attended to. (A.D.Packer)

50. The author makes no apologies for including this view, it is his home tram stop, situated just a few yards past the "Welcome Inn." It can certainly be said that a life long passion was born here on Well Hall Road, watching the big red trams go by. (R.J.Harley Coll.)

51. Nobody at the request stop, so car 565 continues coasting downhill towards Well Hall roundabout. As can be noted in this picture the pre-fabricated homes installed by the LCC in the immediate post war years were an eminently practical solution for housing bombed-out and homeless families. (D.A.Thompson)

52. Those who know the South Circular today will find it incredible that anyone could saunter across like the gentleman in the picture, with only a passing tramcar to worry about. At this spot in 1992 four lines of traffic regularly feature in the rush hour hold ups. (R.J.Harley Coll.)

53. A United Dairies milk tanker emerges from the A2, Rochester Way to pursue car 1174 round Well Hall Circus. That the trees in the middle should have survived so well is nothing short of miraculous as on at least three occasions the roads leading to the roundabout received direct hits from high explosive Luftwaffe bombs. (W.J.Haynes)

54. Rehabilitated car 1587 rounds the curve towards Westhorne Avenue on service 72. Beside Well Hall Road is a row of houses belonging to the Progress Estate which was started for munitions workers in 1915 and handed over to the Royal Arsenal Cooperative Society in 1925. The whole estate is now subject to a preservation order. (D.A.Thompson)

55. Symbolically perhaps car 92 is overtaken by an STL type bus on its way to Eltham, Southend Crescent on 28th June 1952. In a few days the trams will be no more and the area will be invaded by yet more diesel fumes. (National Tramway Museum. R.J.S.Wiseman)

56. In Well Hall Parade an LCC car pauses at a tram stop. On the left is the former Well Hall House which was the residence of famous children's author Edith Nesbit and her husband Hubert Bland. Here they entertained many celebrities including George Bernard Shaw who arrived once on the tram from Woolwich after meeting workers at the Arsenal. (R.J.Harley Coll.)

57. This is Eltham Well Hall station railway bridge with car 100 about to ascend to the town centre. Oddly enough the track in the dip under the bridge still exists as it was tarred over when the trams ceased. This scene has been substantially altered by the Rochester Way Relief Road which now dives under where the tram is standing. (D.A.Thompson)

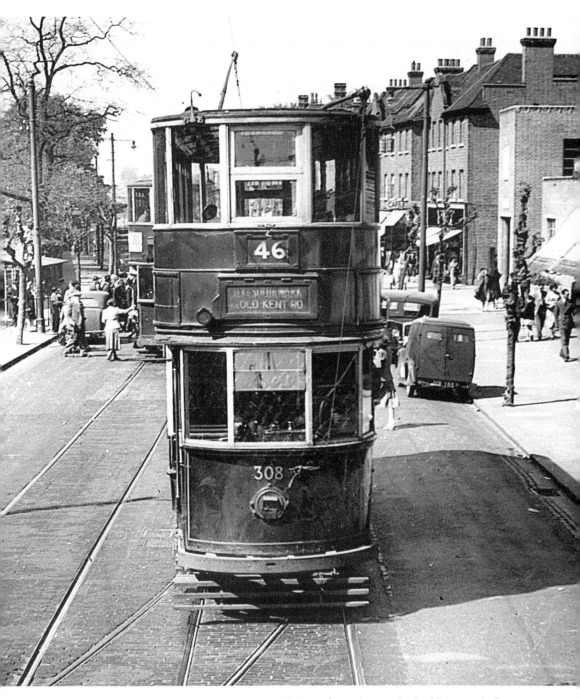

←

58. Nearing the crest of the hill, two ex-West Ham cars pass. One wonders how long the photographer had to wait to compose such a scene. (D.A.Thompson)

59. Seen from the top deck of the tram in front, car 308 approaches the facing crossover outside Eltham Church. Behind an awkwardly placed motor car is surrounded by shoppers boarding a Woolwich bound tram on Saturday, 13th. May 1950.
(National Tramway Museum. H.B.Priestley)

60. It was a less hectic era for some before World War I. Motorman and conductor pose with their charge with St.John's Parish Church in the background. The horse and cart are standing by the section box marking the end of the line. (R.J.Harley Coll.)

61. Forty years later than the previous view the lych gate still stands as a New Cross bound tram glides round the curve into Eltham High Street. (L.Dove)

62. On the afternoon of 29th. August 1944 a doodlebug (Nazi V1 flying bomb) hit the area to the left of the tram causing extensive damage to Hitches' Garage and the church spire. Two people were killed and fifty injured. In quieter times a tram on service 44 heads towards the terminus. (C.Carter)

63. Eltham Hill is the tranquil setting for a view which captures some of the romance of the London tramcar in its final years. (D.A.Thompson)

65. Car 577 was much photographed in the last months of the trams. Here it is negotiating the automatic points on the "Yorkshire Grey" roundabout. (D.A.Thompson)

64. At the bottom of Eltham Hill by the roundabout, John Wills was at hand to record that at 2·15 pm on 14th. April 1952, car 186 on service 46 lost its leading pair of brake magnets which then smashed the plough carrier. Car 577 is about to work wrong road past the obstruction, whilst LT officials ponder the alternatives. However, in those days, "the service must go on" was the paramount philosophy. (A.J.Wills)

66. Westhorne Avenue connects Well Hall Circus with the "Yorkshire Grey" roundabout. It was the LCC's tramway swansong and a projected extension to meet the tram terminus at Grove Park was done to death by bus-mad London Transport. Here we see a car about to pass under the railway bridge by Briset Road. (D.A.Thompson)

67. The broad expanse of Eltham Green breaks up the urban scene. Note the inspector standing by the Eltham Road sign. No doubt, he was keeping a wary eye on the timekeeping of the service 46 car, which was on a depot run to Abbey Wood. (C.Carter)

68. The conductor ties down one of the trolley poles as car 92 is about to reverse. The tram stop sign to the left reads, 44--Alighting Point Only. Sutcliffe Park lies behind the tram and the photographer is standing in front of the "Yorkshire Grey" public house. (D.A.Thompson)

ROUTE 44   **Woolwich - Eltham**   P.M. times are in heavy figures

Via New Road (return via Grand Depot Road), Woolwich Common, Academy Road, Well Hall Road, Eltham Hill.
RAILWAY STATIONS SERVED : Woolwich Arsenal, Eltham Well Hall. Service interval : WEEKDAYS ONLY 6-8 mins. (Sat. aft. and eve. 5 mins.)

	MON. to FRI. First	Last	SATURDAY First	Last			MON. to FRI. First	Last	SATURDAY First	Last
WOOLWICH Beresford Square	5 54	10 12	5 52	10 15	ELTHAM Middle Park Avenue		6 17	10 35	6 15	10 39
Eltham Well Hall Circus	6 6	10 24	6 4	10 27	Eltham Church		6 22	10 38	6 18	10 42
Eltham Church	6 12	10 30	6 10	10 33	Eltham Well Hall Circus	6 10	6 26	10 44	6 34	10 48
ELTHAM Middle Park Avenue	6 15	10 33	6 13	10 36	WOOLWICH Beresford Square	6 22	6 38	10 56	6 36	11 0

ROUTE 46   **Woolwich - Eltham - Lewisham - New Cross - City** *Southwark*   P.M. times are in heavy figures

Via New Rd. (return via Grand Depot Rd.), Woolwich Common, Academy Rd., Well Hall Rd., Eltham Hill, Eltham Rd., Lee Green, Lee High Rd., Loampit Vale, Loampit Hill, Lewisham Way, New Cross Rd., Old Kent Rd., Great Dover Street, Marshalsea Rd., Southwark Bridge Rd., Southwark Bridge
RAILWAY STATIONS SERVED : Woolwich Arsenal, Eltham Well Hall, Lewisham, St. Johns, New Cross Gate, Borough

Service interval : Woolwich-New Cross, MONDAY to FRIDAY 6 minutes (peak hours 3 minutes, evening 4-5 minutes), SATURDAY 6 minutes (peak hours 3 minutes, afternoon and evening 4 minutes), SUNDAY morn. 5 minutes, afternoon and evening 4 minutes. New Cross-City, WEEKDAYS 6 minutes (Mon. to Fri. evening 15 minutes. Sat. afternoon and evening 8 mins.) SUNDAY 10 minutes (afternoon and evening 8 minutes)

	WEEKDAYS First				MON. to FRI. Last		SATURDAY Last		SUNDAY First		Last	
	*	*		SO	MF							
WOOLWICH Beresford Square			4 17	4 37	5 0	5 11	9 48	11 15 11 32	9 49	11 27 11 44	4 43	5 5 5 40 7 10	9 50	11 28 11 32
Eltham Well Hall Circus			4 29	4 49	5 12	5 23	10 0	11 27 11 44	10 0	11 39 11 44	4 55	5 17 5 52 7 22	10 2	11 40 11 44
Eltham Church	4 0		4 35	4 55	5 18	5 29	10 6	11 33 11 50	10 6	11 45 11 50	5 0	5 22 5 57 7 27	10 7	11 45 11 49
Eltham Middle Park Avenue	4 3			4 58	5 21	5 32	10 9	11 36	10 9	11 48		5 25 6 0 7 30	10 10	11 48
Lee Green Tigers Head	4 8			5 3	5 26	5 37	10 14	11 41	10 15	11 54		5 29 6 4 7 34	10 14	11 52
Lewisham Clock Tower	4 15			5 10	5 33	5 44	10 21	11 48	10 23	12 2		6 12 7 42	10 22	12 0
New Cross Gate	4 25	5 11		5 20	5 43	5 54	10 31	11 58	10 33	12 12		6 22 7 52	10 32	12 10
Old Kent Road Bricklayers Arms	4 36	5 22			5 54	6 5	10 42		10 44			8 3	10 43	
CITY Southwark	4 46	5 32			6 4	6 15	10 51		10 53			8 12	10 52	
	*	*		MF	SO									
CITY Southwark				4 51	5 34	5 35	10 56		10 56			8 15	10 56	
Old Kent Road Bricklayers Arms				5 1	5 44	5 45	11 5		11 5			8 24	11 5	
New Cross Gate	3 33	3 42		5 5	5 12	5 55	5 56	11 16 11 32	11 16	11 32		5 32 8 35	11 16	11 32
Lewisham Clock Tower	3 43	3 52		5 15	5 22	6 5	6 6	11 26 11 42	11 26	11 42		5 42 8 45	11 26	11 42
Lee Green Tigers Head	3 50	3 59		5 22	5 29	6 12	6 13	11 34 11 50	11 34	11 50		5 34 5 50 8 53	11 33	11 50
Eltham Middle Park Avenue	3 55	4 4		5 27	5 34	6 17	6 18	11 38 11 54	11 40	11 56		5 38 5 54 8 57	11 38	11 54
Eltham Church	3 58	4 7	4 38	5 30	5 37	6 20	6 21	11 41 11 57	11 43	11 59	5 4	5 41 5 57 9 0	11 41	11 57
Eltham Well Hall Circus		4 13	4 44	5 36	5 43	6 26	6 27	11 47 12 3	11 49	12 5	5 9	5 46 6 2 9 5	11 46	12 2
WOOLWICH Beresford Square		4 25	4 56	5 48	5 55	6 38	6 39	11 59 12 15	12 1	12 17	5 21	5 58 6 14 9 17	11 58	12 14

MF—Monday to Friday only.
SO—Saturday only.
*—Special early journey.

EARLY AND LATE JOURNEYS
Abbey Wood to Woolwich, WEEKDAYS at 4 2, 4 22 a.m.; SUNDAY at 4 28, 4 50 a.m.
Woolwich to Abbey Wood, MON. to FRI. at 11 45, 11 50, 11 55, 11 59 p.m., 12 2, 12 5, 12 7, 12 10, 12 12, 12 15 a.m.; SATURDAY at 5 14, a.m.,
11 49, 11 53, 11 57 p.m. 12 1, 12 5, 12 9, 12 11, 12 13, 12 17 a.m.; SUNDAY at 11 44, 11 48, 11 50, 11 53, 11 58 p.m. 12 4, 12 9, 12 11, 12 14

LEE GREEN

← →

69. Eltham Road, Lee presents a leafy aspect as the motorman of car 100 shuts off power to pass under the section feed, which is indicated by the white bands on the traction standards. (D.A.Thompson)

←

70. This time the trees are bare as car 307 outpaces an East Kent coach outbound from Victoria to the Channel coast. (D.A.Thompson)

71. Lee Green change pit in front of the fire station was a favourite spot with enthusiasts to watch Eltham bound trams "shooting the plough" as the cars sped past. Previous to this the trams would have stopped at the crossroads for the conductor to put up the trolley, after which power was drawn from the overhead. Cars approaching Lewisham, however, would slow to walking pace as the plough was forked into the carrier, then come to a halt as the trolley was hooked down. (C.Carter)

5. Plumstead to Dartford
PLUMSTEAD

72. Our journey east continues. On returning to Beresford Square we take an eastbound car past the Perrott Street crossover where a service 40 tram is about to reverse back to London. (John C. Gillham)

73. Plumstead High Road contained several stretches of single track and passing loops. Car 1877 reaches the double track by Griffin Road trolleybus reverser; trams being double ended avoided the rather ungainly spectacle of being driven backwards into side streets to reverse. (D.A.Thompson)

74. The street sweeper to the left of car 1887 seems unperturbed as the tram swings into the centre of the road. Such antics as this brought the wrath of motoring organisations and town planners on the heads of the tram operators. (D.A.Thompson)

75. Opposite the police station by Riverdale Road was a facing crossover. As can be seen, clearances were very restricted in this part of the High Street. (John C. Gillham)

76. After the junction with the former Bexley tramways at Wickham Lane, the track singled again; here a 698 trolleybus is seen approaching the camera. (John C. Gillham)

77. Car 309 is the centrepiece in a symmetrical arrangement of stop signs and passing loop, as it waits for a tram coming in the other direction. (John H. Meredith)

78. A web of overhead sways gently above car 1826 as it turns into Basildon Road. As the road was wider, there were separate wires for trams and trolleybuses, so that overtaking was possible. (C.Carter)

ABBEY WOOD

79. At the end of the straight run along Mc.Leod Road, car 200 slows for the right angle bend into Knee Hill and Abbey Wood terminus. (Lens of Sutton)

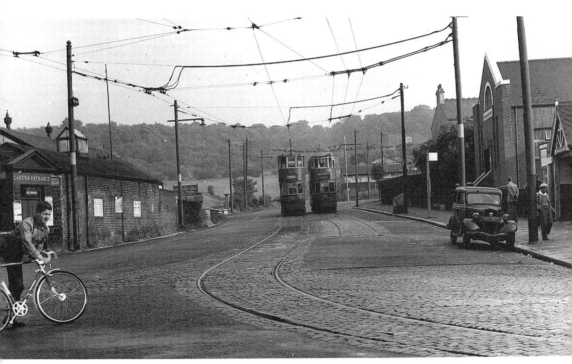

80. Looking south at the quaintly named Knee Hill. The remnants of the Erith connecting curve are to the left of the picture. On the right the track proceeds to Abbey Wood depot. The old county boundary ran right down the centre of the road between the two tracks; we can assume that the photographer had one leg in Kent and the other in London!
(John C. Gillham)

81. Looking north this time, LCC car 1566 has just crossed into Kent and is pausing before the return to Woolwich. The tram carries an EX plate to show it is extra to the normal service; these metal signs were introduced in summer 1912 and were replaced by Venner number stencils in the top deck front window from summer 1913. (R.J.Harley Coll.)

82. A rare view of the Abbey Wood formation tram dancing team rehearsing in the street outside the depot. The picture is dated April 1949, one wonders whether it was the first? Whilst such shunting manoeuvres were an enthusiast's joy, the local residents were probably not so impressed especially early in the morning and late at night. (A.D.Packer)

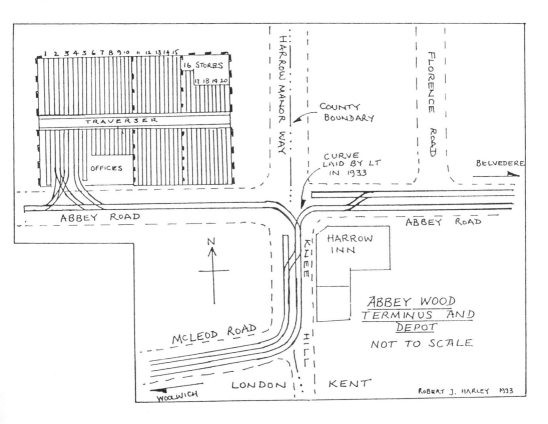

83. The LCC looked upon Erith Council Tramways rather disdainfully and would never agree to a through service; it was left to LT to make the connection in 1933 so that Erith depot could be closed and the local cars shifted to Abbey Wood which had a theoretical capacity of 86 trams, although by the end of tramway operation the figure was nearer 56. Here we see Erith car 13D repainted in LT red and cream swinging into Abbey Road on its way to Bexleyheath. (G.N.Southerden)

36 Blackwall Tunnel—New Bridge St., Blackfriars
via Blackwall Lane, Trafalgar Rd., Greenwich Rd., Deptford Bdwy.,
New X Rd., Old Kent Rd., New Kent Rd., 'Elephant,' & Blackfriars Bg'
THROUGH FARE 3½d.

Weekdays	From Blackwall Tunl.. First Car 5.86 am	Last Car 11.24 pm
	New Bridge St.. 6.6	12.19 am
Sundays	Blackwall Tunl.. 7.54, 8.27	11.19 pm
	New Bridge St.. 8.44, 9.17	12.8 am

38 Chapel St., Woolwich—Waterloo Bg. (Victoria Embk.)
via Woolwich Rd., Trafalgar Rd., Greenwich Rd., Deptford Bdy, New
X Rd., Old Kent Rd., New Kent Rd., 'Elephant,' & Westminster Bg.
THROUGH FARE 4d.

Weekdays	From Chapel St.. First Car 7.11 am	Last Car 10.59 pm
	Waterloo Bg 6.29	10.29
Sundays	Chapel St.. 9.34	11.16
	(8.14 from Blackwall Lane)	
	Waterloo Bg 10.18 am	10.81
	(8.29 from Charing X)	(12.21 to Blackwall Ln)

40 Chapel St., Woolwich—Waterloo Bg. (Victoria Embk.)
via Woolwich Rd., Trafalgar Rd., Greenwich Rd., Deptford, New
X Rd., Peckham, Camberwell New Rd., Kennington Rd., & Wesmr.Bg.
THROUGH FARE 4d.

Weekdays	From Chapel Street.. First Car 4.49 am	Last Car 11.81 pm
	Waterloo Bdg. 5.16	12.7
Sundays	Chapel Street.. 8.87	11.2
	Waterloo Bdg. 8.29	11.44

LCC March 1913

ERITH

84. Two Erith cars in their attractive apple green and cream livery, pass outside the "Halfway House" on the route to Erith town centre. (R.J.Harley Coll.)

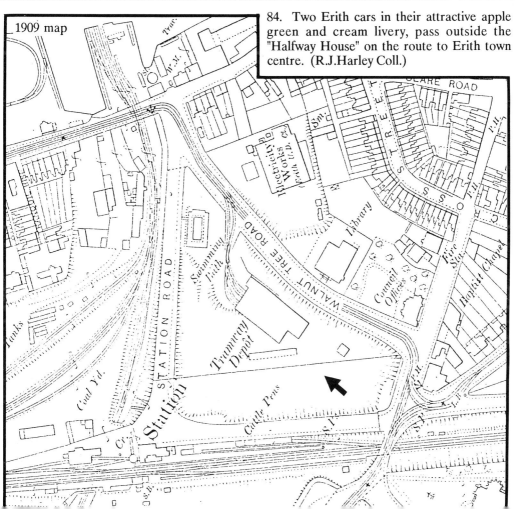

1909 map

85. The driver is probably muttering something about industrial railways holding up the traffic in this West Street scene before World War I. The level crossing was over two lines, both running to wharves on the Thames. One was 4ft gauge from Parrish's Loam Quarry and the other was standard gauge from Vicker's Works. (R.J.Harley Coll.)

86. Still in West Street, an original open top car is seen shortly after the LT take over; by this time the second Erith livery had weathered from a deep maroon to a colour best described as black! (G.N.Southerden)

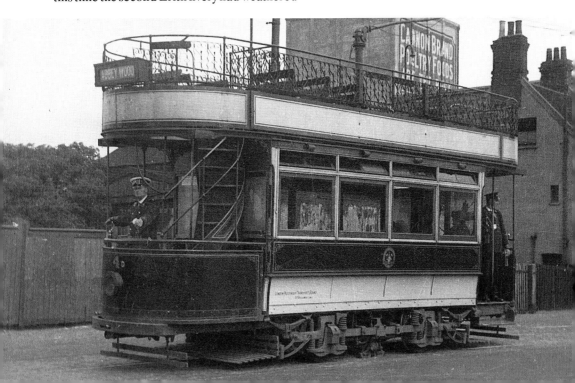

87. The depot was in Walnut Tree Road and outlived the trams by around forty years, until it too fell victim to modern town planning. The fleet looks splendid in this pre-opening scene. (R.J.Harley Coll.)

88. A wonderful example of street furniture is this tram shelter at the triangular junction outside the Wheatley Hotel. An Erith car in original condition heads towards Northumberland Heath. (R.J.Harley Coll.)

89. Passengers waiting at Northumberland Heath were treated to a different style of ornate shelter which reflected civic pride in days gone by. The covered top tram is not proceeding past the photographer into Bexley territory, but has the trolley already turned for the return to Abbey Wood. (R.J.Harley Coll.)

90. Silhouetted against the winter sun an Erith car stops to pick up passengers. The whole scene has an air of the late 1920s about it. Less romantic is the state of the track in the foreground which from the look of it seems to be well worn. (A.J.Watkins)

91. At Bexleyheath Market Place in the summer of 1934 a motorman eyes the camera quizically as he takes one last puff of his cigarette. It is easy to forget how grateful we should be to the pioneers of tramway photography for preserving a way of life on film. (A.B.Cross)

LCC March 1913

44 BERESFORD SQ., Woolwich—ELTHAM.
via Woolwich Common Road, and Well Hall Road.
THROUGH FARE **2**d.

				Last Car 11.30 pm
Weekdays	From Beresford Square..First Car 5.0 am			11.49
	Eltham	5.20		
Sundays	Beresford Square..	8.30		11.25
	Eltham	8.50		11.45

46 LEE GREEN—WATERLOO STATION.
via Lewisham, New X. Peckham, Walworth Road, & 'Elephant.'
THROUGH FARE **3½**d.

			Last Car 11.51 pm
Weekdays	From Lee Green ..First Car 4.58 am		11.39(12.40 to New X)
	Waterloo Stn.	5.40	11.30 pm
Sundays	Lee Green ..	8.58	11.35 (12.17 to Lewisham
	Waterloo Stn.	8.32	

48 LEE GREEN—VICTORIA STATION.
via Lewisham, New Cross, Camberwell Green, Camberwell New Road, and Vauxhall.
THROUGH FARE **4**d.

				Last Car 11.7 pm
Weekdays	From Lee Green ..First Car 7.1 am			11.45
	Victoria ..	7.51		
Sundays	Lee Green ..	10.4		11.3
	Victoria ..	10.51		11.25

50 CATFORD—GREENWICH CHURCH.
via Lewisham Road and South Street.
THROUGH FARE **1½**d.

			Last Car 11.45 pm
Weekdays	From Catford ..First Car 5.0 am		(12.25 to South Street)
	Greenwich Church	4.55	12.4 am
Sundays	Catford ..	8.6	11.42 pm
			(12.22 to South Street)
	Greenwich Church	8.23	12.1 am

92. Towards the end of its career, Bexley B class car 28 stops at the passing loop in a deserted Broadway. The business of A.Hide & Co. was founded in 1851 and the shop behind the tram was modernised in 1936 and further rebuilt in the 1950s. The whole block was torn down in 1979 to make way for yet another ugly shopping mall. (R.Elliott)

93. Tramway networks in action! Bexley car 16 still carries its original oil headlamp whilst Dartford car 2 waits to depart for Horns Cross. (R.J.Harley Coll.)

94. Further along the Broadway, LT car 1717 passes the entrance to Bexley tram depot. These M class cars were transferred back into the area to replace the original local trams which were falling to pieces. The track and overhead were also in pretty poor shape, and LT gave strict instructions that no tram was to be driven faster than half speed because of the risk of derailment. (R.J.Harley Coll.)

95. Municipal enterprise having seen better days, could be the caption. By the early 1930s a general air of make do and mend settled on the undertaking and no doubt the flat truck on the centre track was in some demand for carting around sections of old rail to keep the service going. (A.J.Watkins)

→

96. In its dying days the depot ressembled a modeller's fiddle yard, with bits and pieces lying everywhere. A sign for the future is the LT tower wagon parked by the tram; it was engaged on rewiring and repoling the route for trolleybuses. (A.B.Cross)

42 ABBEY WOOD—FREE FERRY, Woolwich.
via McLeod Road, Plumstead Road, and Beresford Square.
THROUGH FARE 2d.

Weekdays	From Abbey Wood..First Cars 4.19, 4.57 am	Last Car 11.38 pm
	Free Ferry .. 5.8	12.3 am
Sundays	Abbey Wood.. 7.50 am	11.54 pm
	Free Ferry .. 8.15	12.17 am

LCC March 1913

97. The crew are enjoying a chat as car 4 enters a passing loop between the depot and Gravel Hill. From the look of the lady on the top deck the temperature wasn't that warm.
(A.J.Watkins)

98. A characteristic of Kentish tramways was the rural nature of some of the routes; with not a single house in sight, an M class car bounces along the country highway. This is the summer of 1935 and new poles are already in place for the replacing trolleybuses. (A.B.Cross)

99. London Road, Crayford and the chap on the delivery bike is peddling fast to keep up with the tram. The gas works are behind the wall on the left. (A.J.Watkins)

100. A bird's eye view of Elm Loop from one of the gasometers, note that the tram is one of the batch fitted with only one trolley pole. (R.J.Harley Coll.)

101. It is the summer of 1906 and Dartford car 8 turns into Crayford High Street. In the centre window is a poster which reads "Through Running. Market Place. Bexleyheath." This service commenced on 27th. August that year. (R.J.Harley Coll.)

102. The Dartford tram in all its splendour with a fine looking motorman to match. No wonder that in the early days, trams were regarded as a transport necessity for every modern borough. (R.J.Harley Coll.)

DARTFORD

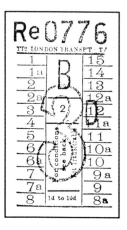

103. Outside the schools in Dartford Road car 1725 looks immaculate in its new livery. On the rocker panel is a notice informing the public that as from 3rd. October 1934 the service will be numbered 96. (C.Carter)

The maps are from 1909 and show the depot (top), which was north-east of the railway station, and the town centre (bottom).

104. There is an old world charm about the centre of the Kentish market town of Dartford. A gentleman in a boater is standing outside the Bull Hotel which is an old coaching inn, whilst a pair in flat caps pass on the other side, clutching bags of chips. Bexley car 28 emerges from Spital Street in the noonday sunshine of either a summer Sunday or a Bank Holiday. There was a three way junction to the right of the tram outside the shuttered David Greig shop. Behind the photographer the tracks divided again for the short branch to Wilmington and the main line to Horns Cross. (A.J.Watkins)

105. A Bank Holiday proved fatal for the Dartford tramways as during the night of 6th./7th. August 1917 the whole fleet, including the cars pictured here, went up in flames. Many local factories were vital for the war effort and the area could not be left without public transport. Fortunately, Bexley stepped in and with the help of a number of hired LCC trams, a service was started on 9th. August. (R.J.Harley Coll.)

→

106. A wartime scene out at Horns Cross with a training run for conductresses. The motorman doesn't look too impressed! (R.J.Harley Coll.)

107. The "Welcome All" public house must have lived up to its name when the biting winter gales swept across Horns Cross tram terminus. Truly this was a London tramway outpost, the furthest east on the system. Note the Maidstone and District bus on its way to Gravesend and Rochester. (A.J.Watkins)

6. Rolling Stock

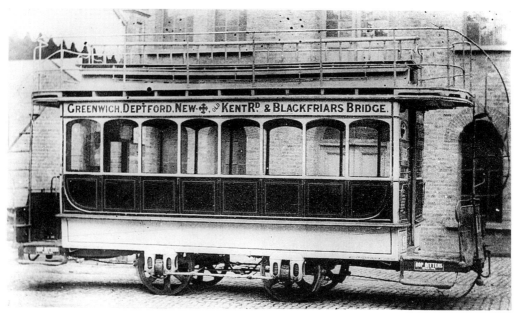

108. Dated September 1882, this is one of the early horse cars which plied the route from Greenwich to the capital. The livery was probably dark blue and white. Horse drawn ambulance trams also operated around Joyce Green Hospital in Dartford; the first section was opened in May 1897 and the track gauge was four feet. The tramway ceased working in 1936 with the rails lifted in 1943.
(National Tramway Museum)

109. LCC B class car 106 has been painstaking-
ly restored by the LCC Tramways Trust and is
seen here at the National Tramway Museum.
The livery is maroon lake and cream, with
trucks and undergear painted red oxide.
(R.J.Harley)

110. A passenger's eye view of the driving
platform of car 106. Notice the shaped wooden
benches, the bulkhead door and the LCC fare
chart. (R.J.Harley)

Most London tramcars were classified into
car types by the use of class letters. The system
was continued by LT after the 1933 takeover.
Each area described in this series of books will
have a similar section devoted to different
types associated with that area. In this volume
we deal with the fleets of the three municipal
operators and look at the LCC B and M class
cars which were used on local routes.

LCC "M" class car.

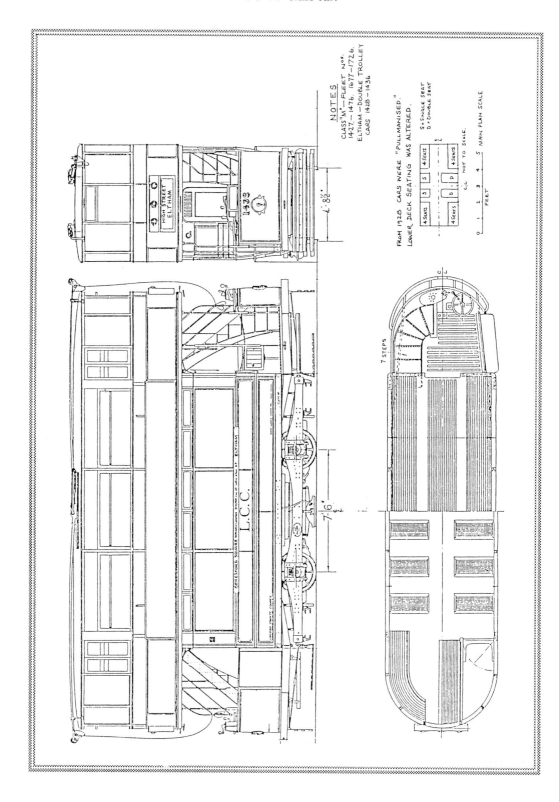

NOTES
CLASS "M" — FLEET Nos.
1427.—1476. 1677—1726.
ELTHAM — DOUBLE TROLLEY
CARS 1428—1436

FROM 1928 CARS WERE "PULLMANISED".
LOWER DECK SEATING WAS ALTERED.

S = SINGLE SEAT
D = DOUBLE SEAT

MAIN PLAN SCALE
0 1 2 3 4 5
FEET

NOT TO SCALE.

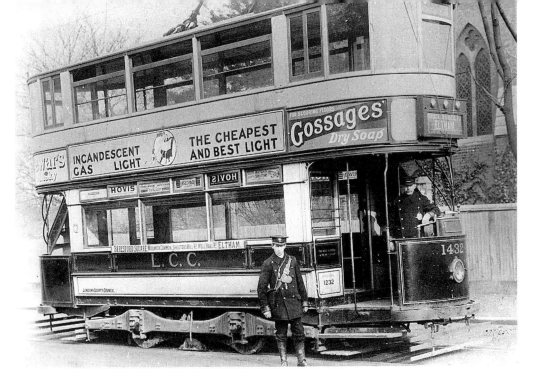

111. The LCC M class first arrived for the Eltham route in 1910. They were mounted on an unusual swing bolster truck which imparted a very distinctive floating motion to the rest of the tram. Cars 1428 to 1437 were equipped with double trolleys and worked service 44 to Eltham Church. (National Tramway Museum)

112. Seen here at Overy Liberty in Dartford, M class car 1700 wears the later LT livery. The fleet numbers of the class were 1428 to 1476 and 1677 to 1726. Many of the class were drafted back into the area to replace worn out Bexley and Erith cars; three survived at Abbey Wood depot until the war years. (C.Carter)

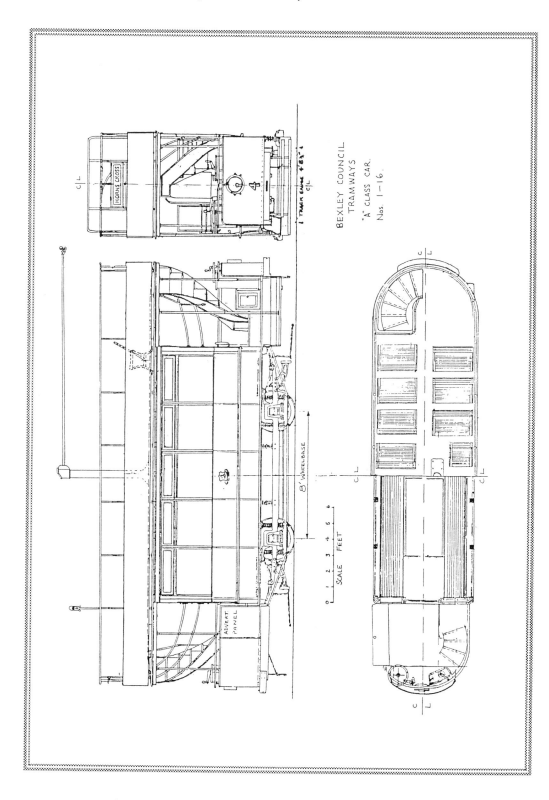

BEXLEY COUNCIL
TRAMWAYS
"A" CLASS CAR.
Nos. 1—16.

HORNS CROSS

ADVERT.
PANEL

8' WHEELBASE

4' 8½" TRACK GAUGE

0 1 2 3 4 5 6
SCALE FEET

113. The Bexley A class cars were built at Preston in 1903 and received new Peckham Pendulum trucks in 1913. Fleet numbers were 1 to 16. The original Bexley livery was maroon and cream; after 1917 cars were painted chocolate and cream. (A.J.Watkins)

Bexley Council Tramways. "B" class car. ('Ex LCC Tramways)

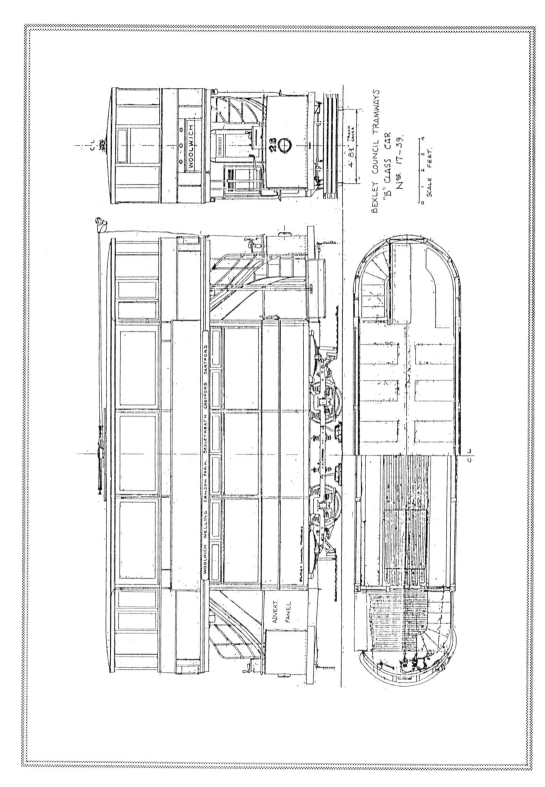

BEXLEY COUNCIL TRAMWAYS
"B" CLASS CAR
Nº. 17–39.

SCALE FEET.

4' 8½" TRACK GAUGE

WOOLWICH

28

WOOLWICH WELLING DANSON PARK BEXLEYHEATH CRAYFORD DARTFORD

ADVERT. PANEL

114. The Bexley B class, fleet numbers 17 to 39, were purchased second hand from the LCC. All had their conduit gear removed and a trolley mounted on the roof. (R.Elliott)

Dartford Council Tramways. Car 2.

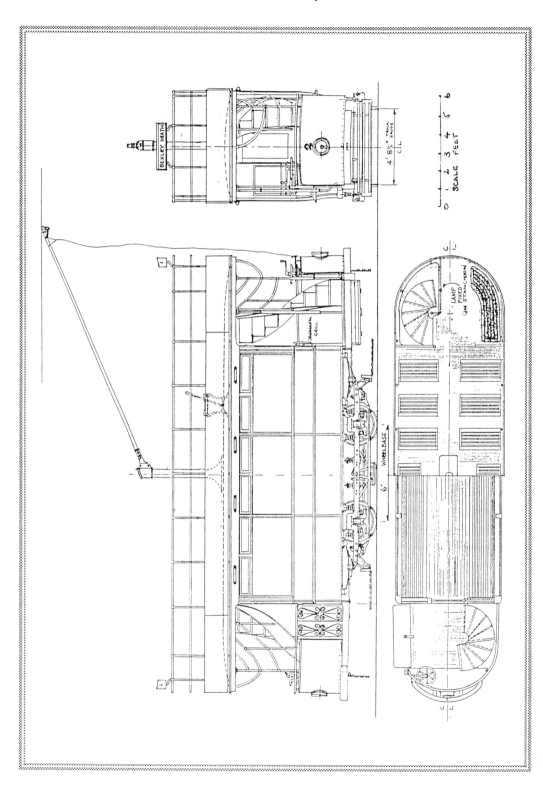

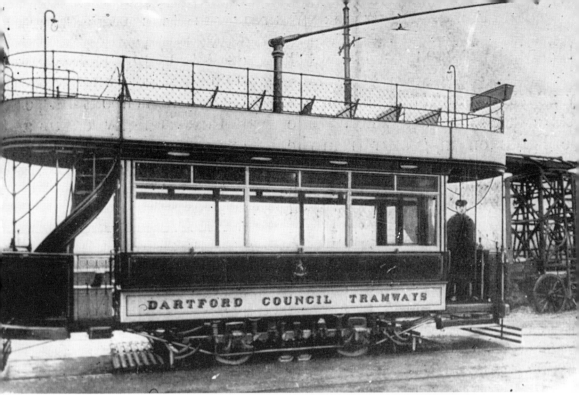

115. Dartford Council cars 1 to 12 were basically the standard British four wheel open top car on Brill 21E trucks. The Dartford livery was a bright maroon and cream. (National Tramway Museum)

116. Erith cars 1 to 6 and car 9 were built by Brush at Loughborough They survived until 1934. (R.J.Harley Coll.)

London Transport (Ex-Erith) car 10D.

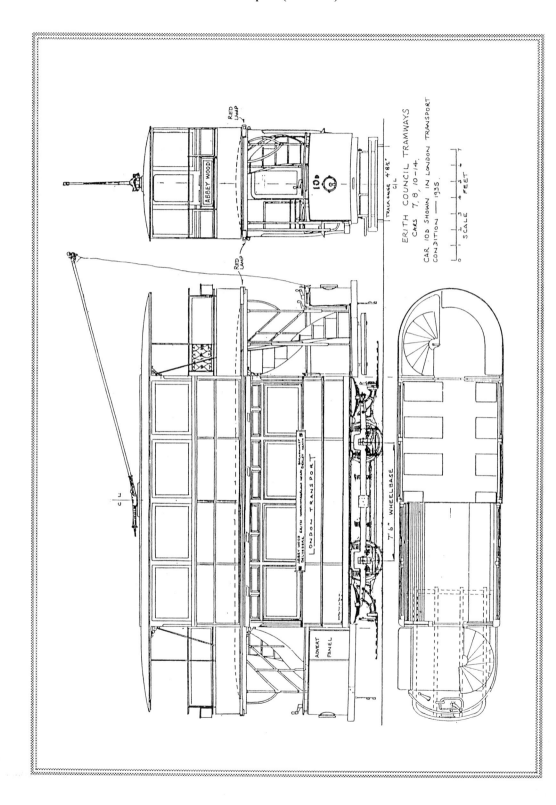

ERITH COUNCIL TRAMWAYS
CARS 7, 8, 10-14.
CAR 10D SHOWN IN LONDON TRANSPORT
CONDITION — 1935.

SCALE FEET

117. Fleet numbers 7,8 and 10 to 14 were covered top versions of the 1 to 6 batch. All Erith cars were retrucked after World War I and on passing to London Transport, the covered cars were placed on ex-Croydon trucks and repainted in the Board's livery. They then survived until the end of tramway operation in 1935. (R.J.Harley Coll.)

118. Pictures of the other Erith trams are rare. Here is car 19 acquired in 1916 from Hull Corporation and promptly christened the "tank" by the staff! Erith also possessed two single deck demi-cars, numbers 15 and 16, four ex-London United bogie cars, numbers 15 to 18(second series) and a water car number 20. (R.J.Harley Coll.)

7. Finale

119. In 1935 publicity material for the new trolleybuses and the brand new depot at Bexleyheath began to appear in the local press. This view shows a B class Leyland on the official opening 10th. November 1935. The trolleybuses were a great success and passenger figures rose; there was much grumbling when LT embarked on another money wasting exercise and replaced the trolleybuses with diesels in 1959. The other Greenwich and Woolwich tramways had also suffered the same fate earlier in the decade. (C.F.Klapper Coll.)

120. Car 144, having just shot its plough, is pushed by the work's tractor towards its final resting place. Lines of its fellows wait in the yard for their fate at the Penhall Road "Tramatorium". (C.Carter)

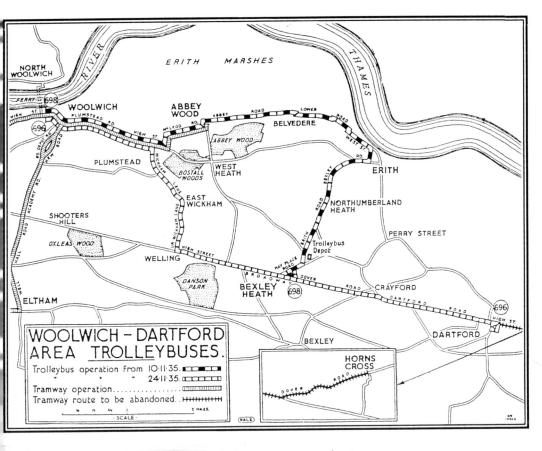

WOOLWICH – DARTFORD AREA TROLLEYBUSES.

Trolleybus operation from 10·11·35.
" " 24·11·35.

Tramway operation................
Tramway route to be abandoned...

· SCALE ·

(HALE)

HORNS CROSS